Digital Connections

Engaging the Always Connected Audience

Jason Caston

Published by Composio Inc.

ISBN-13:

Edited by: Candice Lowe - Composio Inc.

Cover Design: Cory Broussard - Composio Inc. and Artistic Embodiment -

http://aembodiment.com

DEDICATION

I dedicate this book to family and friends.To my kids who finally realized Dad writes books and speaks on stage… to my mom and sisters who support everything I do and know that I put family over everything. And to serendipity (the occurrence and development of events by chance in a happy or beneficial way), something about it changed my whole outlook, she is amazing.

TABLE OF CONTENTS

CHAPTER 1 - THINK DIGITAL

Introduction

When I speak or teach, I always start out by saying the same thing, which is to first let my audience know that my goals for the day are to layout a template that will give them some best practices for establishing an effective online presence. Secondly, that I want to teach them quite a few key areas to focus on for their digital presence, as well as give them the tools and instructions to go back and implement what we discussed. Lastly, I share that I want to give them a glimpse of what's coming in the future of digital. I realize that digital platforms are evolving rapidly and if I don't let them know what's coming, then they will be behind the curve quickly. Well that's the goal of this book, to do those exact things and more. I am not saying this book will be your go-to manual for every topic addressed, but we will touch on different digital areas and give you some insight on how and why to use these tools and channels.

For the last 10 years or so, I have been helping organizations connect with, engage and grow their online audiences. When I first started, it was the norm for organizations to create digital platforms in silos. The website was its own thing, social media was just a place to post stuff, mobile was just to make sure the website was responsive and build apps, and the whole focus of eCommerce was to make money, followed by the multimedia of video and audio files that were put online... somehow. Each of these things operated independently of each other and their focus was outward marketing and not engagement. But I did start to see the pieces come together and I started to see ways that the website, multimedia, eCommerce, social media and mobile could all come together in a cohesive digital strategy that any organization could use to grow online. I called this five-part methodology the iChurch Method because I was working with churches at that time. Since then, the methodology has grown to include more parts, but the foundation is the same, which is you need a digital strategy.

Think Digital

I've noticed an interesting trend that is arising amongst organizations when it comes to reaching people online -- they are very one-track minded. When it comes to developing a strategy to grow their online audience, social media is the all-encompassing solution. Many organizations believe that if you throw some social media stuff at it (posts, graphics, maybe a video) then it will reach people online and have an impact. Is this your organization? Does your leadership believe that social media is the answer to all your online outreach/marketing problems? Well trust me, your organization is not alone, but there's an answer that's even better than just social media.

While social media is a great piece of the online outreach pie, there are other pieces that are still necessary to reach, engage and grow your online audience. The answer to this issue is that organizations need to "Think Digital" and not just "Social". Thinking Digital means that you need to have a full digital strategy for your organization. A full digital strategy looks like all the ways that your organization connects with people in the online space. Usually, this consists of social, mobile, web, eCommerce, multimedia and more.

As society continues to blur the lines of offline and online, I believe that the most important aspects of any digital strategy are social and mobile. Let me explain, for the last 10 years, social has driven mobile growth and mobile has driven social growth. Here's a perfect example: Facebook's social features made us want to connect with it, but it's mobile features gave it the ability to connect with us, anywhere, anytime, anyplace.

Let's look at how to be more focused on growing our online platforms and increasing engagement with our online audiences. While there is no shortage of ways to do this, it seems that creating an online strategy is quite elusive for many organizations. One of the most important aspects of building an online presence for your organization is to develop a digital strategy, *"before"* you join any networks or start communicating online. This strategy includes:

- Gathering the content from different departments within your organization
- Organizing the team that will help gather, distribute the content and interact with your online audience
- Determining which platforms you will utilize to get this content out to the masses and connect with people online

Do Churches Understand the Digital Experience?

We often hear church attendance is declining. Pew Research Group has done numerous studies that back these statements. But for church communicators, we believe something different is occurring. It's not that church attendance is declining, it's that church attendance is decentralizing.

What I mean by decentralizing is simple: rather than people physically attending, many are connecting digitally to their churches. Because of that, many people would say it is no longer about how many people you get into the building, but how many you engage with—regardless of the platform.

This is why a good digital experience (web, social, mobile, eCommerce, etc.) is so crucial to modern churches.

What makes a good digital experience? It is not as complex as it sounds. It begins with the idea of ecosystems then branches out from there.

Connectivity and Cohesive Experiences - Focus on Ecosystems

Many churches understand that experiences do not occur in the sanctuary alone. The church's ministries must be in line with her mission, creating a consistent experience. Interaction—whether that is from the pastor's message, the men's ministry event, or children's program—is best supported by consistent branding, messaging, and communication of the gospel and the church's mission. The offline ecosystem of the church is established well and has been for years. Unfortunately, many churches fail to see this consistency is necessary in the online life of the church, too. Church culture has to be consistent in the digital space as much as it does in the real world. Every church needs to understand its digital ecosystem.

Digital Ecosystems

Digital ecosystems are all about consistency, connectivity, and the results of that connectivity. We can think of Apple, Google, Amazon and Facebook for examples of great ecosystems. For these companies, the online experience, message, and branding is consistent across their platforms. You never feel like you have left their ecosystem and thus you start to associate their online presence with a positive experience.

In the church digital ecosystem, your website is the core. It is the home base of your mission and message. From there the system spreads outward via social media (Facebook, etc.), apps, and other multimedia channels (YouTube, and so on). If your church community is to benefit most, the experience, branding, and messages should be as consistent as they are in the physical church and its ministries—or perhaps even more. As modern digital media experts advise, it also "means that in order to make an impact in [church members'] lives, you need to have a system for reaching consumers on every device (mobile, tablets, TV, computers)." When you wish to speak to specific people across multiple platforms, they must have a consistent experience of the church and must be able to easily remain connected via that ecosystem.

All of this is also known as an omni-channel experience. This experience serves your church in a deep and meaningful way. But it is also an integrated and cohesive manner, no matter how church members reach out. If your church strategy does not involve the creation of this cross-platform or omni-channel experience, you may see your church decline rather than simply decentralize. That is an avoidable path and one that starts by looking at your church's digital experience with the same seriousness as you do the physical one.

CHAPTER 2 - DIGITAL MARKETING

What is Digital Marketing?

According to Hubspot Digital, marketing encompasses all marketing efforts that use an electronic device or the internet. Businesses leverage digital channels such as search engines, social media, email, and other websites to connect with current and prospective customers. Digital marketing is defined by the use of numerous digital tactics and channels to connect with customers where they spend much of their time: online.

The key to digital marketing is to reach customers where they are at. Take the message to them on the platforms they are already using. Whether it's paid ads on Google, Facebook and Instagram, or it's content marketing on your blog or Medium.com, there are multiple channels to reach customers where they are. Every day there are new platforms, channels and technologies that evolve the way we communicate and connect with each other. These new platforms are now becoming some of the most effective digital marketing channels in history.

WIth these new platforms we are seeing users want an omni-channel experience, which means the same experience no matter the digital channel. User experiences that start on social can continue via mobile and also on the web. Users want all of your platforms to have consistent experiences, meaning no matter how they connect with you, they want it to look and feel similar. If the experience is familiar and similar, then users can focus on the campaign's message and story, which we will discuss next.

The key is developing a campaign that takes an impactful message, wraps it in a great story, gives a clear call-to-action, uses multiple channels and measures the results. When developing a digital marketing strategy you want to find the intersection of your audience's pain points and your solution. Identify how your product or service will help make their lives better and then you start developing your message around that.

Here is an example of a strategy that I have used in the past. When creating a digital strategy, we looked at the website, online store and online giving, social media, mobile and multimedia channels. We decided that across all these channels we would have a strategy that consisted of Inspiration, Education, Information, Communication, Diversification and Consistency.

- <u>Inspiration</u> - Inspire your audience with your content, make them feel as if they can be better than they currently are, based on your content. How will your products or services inspire them to better themselves?

- <u>Education</u> - Educate your audience on how your products or services will solve their problems and make their lives better. Identify the pain points that your audience has and educate them on solutions. Once they understand the possible solutions, then guide them to how your products and services will do just that... provide the solution!

- <u>Information</u> - Keep your audience informed on the events and happenings within your organization. People today want to feel connected to an organization, and while you are running a business, people connect with people. Thus, try to make your content feel like it's coming from a person to connect with another person.

- <u>Communication</u> - Every platform encourages and rewards communication. Whether it's social media, video platforms like YouTube, blogging platforms like Medium or elsewhere, when someone comments on your page or sends you a message, best practice is to respond. Now, this does not include the nonsense messages or the vitriol that is always a part of the internet comments. I am talking about genuine people who either have commented on your content (photos, videos, text, etc.) or people who are using your social media channels as customer service channels and want to tell you how great you are or ask for help in resolving an issue. Effective and efficient communication is a great strategy to use for your company.

- Diversification - Many times I have taught and I always let companies know, don't just use Facebook for your social media strategy. I have seen pages with millions of fans get taken down for numerous reasons and the companies cannot do anything about it because it's technically not their platform, it belongs to the social media company that created it. Therefore, whether it's social media or multimedia or other platforms, don't put all your eggs in one platform's basket. If your organization is on social media then be on multiple platforms (Facebook, Instagram, Twitter). If you are on YouTube then also consider Vimeo. But no matter how many platforms you are on, the main platform you should have for any digital marketing strategy is your website. Your website is your homebase, it's where your strategies should funnel your audience to.

- Consistency - Be consistent in your digital marketing execution. Don't start marketing on any channels that you cannot be consistent on. Don't start a monthly newsletter that you will not be able to maintain after the first two months. Don't start using social media and then go silent for six months and not post anything. Make sure that any channels you use for social remain consistent in engaging its audience.

This six part strategy guided the type of content we created and how we distributed that content to our channels based on what the goals of our campaign was. So once we have content created and we have a strategy, then we need to look at a few channels we can use, and that's what we get into next.

Channels

- Content Marketing - Content marketing consists of the creation of content that's used to generate awareness, growth, lead generation and of course customers. This type of content is usually blogs, ebooks, whitepapers, case studies and infographics. Blogs are short-form content that ranges from impersonal company updates that keep your audience informed to professional posts that showcase your companies expertise. Likewise, ebooks, whitepapers and case studies are considered more long-form content that helps educate your audience on your companies products, services and areas of expertise. Each of these items help the customer understand how their problems can be solved via your products and/or services. Lastly, infographics are a visual representation of these same concepts. Many times people want to see a more visual representation of your content, and infographics are a great example of this.

- Online Ads - Online advertising, also referred to as PPC (pay-per-click) marketing is one of the most effective ways to generate traffic and grow awareness for your brand. Quick sidenote, when someone says organic traffic, they are referring to FREE traffic that came without using ads. Online ads include Facebook, Instagram, Twitter, YouTube, Google, LinkedIn and so much more. These are a few of the platforms where you can invest in online ads and pay-per-click or per impression and get a good return of investment. The key to online ads is two-fold, first you need to identify your target audience. You can customize your target audience on these platforms so if you want to target married women between the ages of 30 - 45, who have children and live in the USA, then you can do that. The more specific you are in your target, the better. Secondly, you need to have a great piece of content for your ad. Whether it's a graphic, video or just text, the quality of your ad is important so make sure you choose it accordingly and test different versions to compare results.

- Email Marketing - Email has been and still remains one of the most effective marketing channels. While spam filters have gotten better and open rates fluctuate, email is still a great marketing tool and is one of the main communication platforms for people in business and personal. Types of email marketing tools are newsletters, follow-up emails, welcome emails, promotional emails, abandoned cart emails and email series/courses. The key to email marketing is coming up with an amazing subject line to get people to open your email, as well as having a balanced mix of text and images in your email.

Sometimes spam filters flag emails with too many images (or all images) and sent them to the spam folder. I've also read studies where all text emails do very well and make things easier for the user to read. Again, test different formats to see which works for your audience and then adapt accordingly.

Conference / Event Strategy - Three Phase Approach

I am often asked how to market a conference. I have worked at-and been to events that had thousands of attendees and I have been to events that didn't have many attendees at all. The difference in these events was not the content/topics of the event, it was the marketing of the event. Marketing of a conference plays a key role in its success and unfortunately, not many people understand this. But here is an example strategy:

<u>Phase 1 - Before the Conference</u>

- Setup Hashtag for Conference
  - Start marketing it on Twitter and Instagram with Save the Date Memes

- Promote conference main product with every registration (this could be a book, t-shirt, etc.)
  - Add cost of item into conference price and include it in the swag bag for attendees

- Create Mobile app and promote download of app

- Purchase Facebook/Twitter ads to promote conference.
    - Ads can be pic/video of main speakers targeted toward that speakers core audience

- Content Marketing
    - Topical Blog posts on website/medium/Facebook Notes and LinkedIn that tie in the speaker's topic

- Speakers Co-Marketing the Conference
    - Setup preset Tweets / Facebook Posts with graphics and hashtag

- Facebook Live Event about Conference with topics related to conference

- Social Media Campaign
    - Promote five things to do in the host city while at the conference (downtown tourist attractions)
    - Top five reasons to attend conference and how it will benefit attendees and their business or make their lives better
    - Video trailers for conference that can go on all platforms

        - If possible use teachings/content from previous year with key quotes and have a call-to-action to register

- Create Group Campaigns
    - For people who bring five or more people
    - Discount ticket price and package deals

Phase 2 - At the Conference

- Mobile App Strategy
    - Live Streaming capabilities
    - Schedule of events
    - Speaker bios and social media channels

- Social Media Strategy
    - Posting schedule of speakers, events and products
    - Live Tweeting of Keynote speakers
    - Taking quotes of speakers and photos and turning them into memes quickly for distribution
    - Promotion of live streaming
    - Promotion of products (onsite and digital)

- Web Strategy

  - Live Streaming

- Sales Strategy
  - DVDs / CDs / MP3s / MP4s of speakers
  - Clothing and other products to sell

Phase 3 - After the Conference

- Thank You Graphics with call-to-action to register for next year's event at a discount
- Product promotions from the event
- Speakers video clips with call-to-action to purchase products
- Memes with quotes and a call-to-action to purchase products

CHAPTER 3 - WEB CONNECTIONS

Think of your website as the foundation or homebase, on which everything else in your digital strategy emanates from. Very similar to how the Pentagon is the homebase of our military strategies and all major decisions are sent to and disseminate from there. Your website should function in the same manner. Your website is not just a place for information anymore, it should be an interactive, immersive online experience. Additionally, it should be the start of an omni-channel experience, the cornerstone of your online ecosystem.

When you connect to Facebook, Amazon, Google, or Apple, you know that you are on their properties. Their homebase is their website and from there they build out their digital strategy. No matter what platform you are on within their digital ecosystem, you feel like you are connected with their brand. That's the premise I want you to have when you think about your website. Think about how you can make this digital platform more interactive and immersive. Also, think about how every campaign, digital platform or other marketing strategy you implement, needs to drive people back to your website in some way.

Quick Note on Church Websites

Everytime I teach a faith-based group on what people are looking for, I reiterate these six key pages.

1. Location - Where are you located? Please make that easy to find.

2. Service times - What time(s) are your services? You may know this information, but new visitors do not.

3. Ministries / Missions - What are your ministries that people can get involved in? Also, do you have children or youth ministries?

4. Giving - Make it easy-to-find and easy-to-give. Don't make it a five step process. Two-to-three steps maximum. If in doubt, look at how easy it is to checkout on Amazon. How many steps does that take? Not many.

5. Messages / Sermons - Making your messages available to watch online is a great way for people to stay connected to your ministry. Everyone can't and won't make it every weekend to your onsite services, so making the messages available to watch later is a great option.

6. Welcome / I am New - It's a good idea to have a page that serves as a welcome or introduction to the church. In this area, you walk your guest through your church and let them quickly see or discover more about you.

SEO - Search Engine Optimization

Google.com is the most visited website on the internet. Most people will not go past the first page of results and if they do, they very rarely go past the second. So in today's society of people who want results now, it's important that your organization's website is on the first page of results. The best way to get your website the most visibility on Google is to make sure it's Search Engine Optimized.

Search Engine Optimization is the process of optimizing your website to rank higher in the search results. Here are some things you can do to increase your SEO:

- Make sure to use certain keywords that people are searching for on your website
- Include H1 and H2 tags (one h1 per page and 2-3 h2 tags) that showcase titles and topics that are relevant to your products or services
- Backlinks (links from other high ranking sites to yours) are great for SEO. If your organization publishes blogs or any content on other platforms, then make sure you link back to your website.

- Tech updates you should make are things such as: making sure your website is mobile responsive, your images are compressed, css files, which are cascading style sheets that format the contents of your webpages, are optimized and that your website loads quickly.

Web Strategy Over Web Pretty

When putting a website together, the usual thought process is to create something that looks great. If a website is old then it just needs a new design, something fresh and new. Unfortunately, that thought process is like taking an old junk car and just putting a new paint job on it and calling it new, with zero regard for the old engine or the broken transmission. When you are creating a new website, you have to have a web strategy. We need to focus on web strategy over web pretty. You should ask yourself, will the website get people where they want to go? Will it give them the information that they want to receive? Do we keep our web content fresh so that it keeps users engaged and coming back? Does our website load quickly, like within 2-3 seconds? Fun fact, for every two seconds it takes your website to load, 50% of your audience leaves, therefore in four seconds you have lost 75% of your original audience.

Ninety-four percent of people will form an instant negative opinion of your business if your website runs slow, functions terribly, is poorly designed or is outdated. Your website is most often the first connection people make with your business and if it's not a great representation, then your business will have to be that much better to overcome a bad website.

Tell Your Story

Your website should tell your story. Whether it's your brand's story, your organization's story or your product/service story, your website should tell a story along with the information that people need. There are many ways to tell this story using different types of content, such as video, text, graphics and more. Which brings me to a point, it's not 2015 anymore my friends, we must let the rotating banners on websites go. Studies have shown that people don't scroll/watch past the second banner so there's no need for them. Instead you should use hero images and hero videos that showcase your company when people get to your site. If you have a lot going on and were used to using banners to show those events, then look at different types of panels or squares to showcase those things. Also, when you are coming up with the pages for your site, make sure that people can get anywhere within 2-3 clicks. Don't bury stuff on the website so people have to set up a rescue team to find the missing content. You can make things a lot easier by having a search bar on your website or a footer sitemap, similar to what is on apple.com.

Analytics

In order to have an effective web strategy, you need to analyze your results, optimize what you are doing well, remove what is not working, and repeat the implementation process. Many organizations don't analyze their website analytics and just "hope" things will work online. That approach is an exercise in futility. If you have the tools to measure your online effectiveness, why not use it to your benefit? Google Analytics is a great tool to measure website effectiveness, and it is free to use.

Google Analytics is very effective in showing your website's online impact. Questions such as "how many visitors your website receives each day", "which pages they visit", and "how long they stay", are answered by web analytics. With information from web analytics, you can make adjustments on your site and improve the user's experience. Web analytics can be obtained for free by using software such as Google Analytics (http://www.google.com/analytics).

Here are some key metrics you want to look at in your Google Analytics:

- Pageviews - The total number of pages viewed. This number includes repeated views of a single-page. In other words, a single-person may view the same page several times, and each view is counted as a pageview.

- Unique Pageviews - The number of individual people who have viewed a specific page at least once during a visit. For example, if a single-user views a page more than once during the same visit, only the original view is counted (whereas general Pageviews count each visit). The Unique Pageviews metric counts each page URL + Page Title combination.

- Average Time on Page - The average amount of time users spend viewing a specific page, screen, or set of pages or screens.

- Bounce Rate - The percentage of single-page visits, or the number of visits in which people left your website from the same page they entered on. For example, if you visit a single-article or page on a website and leave, that's counted as a bounce and is factored into the Bounce Rate.

- Percentage Exit - The percentage of users who exit from a page or set of pages.

- Behavior Flow This will let you know the pages users visit on your website, the links they click-on, and what pages they exit your website from.

- Site Content - This will let you know which pages are most popular on your website and which ones are not being viewed at all.

- Site Speed - Google now ranks pages according to how long it takes them to load and download while people are browsing your website. Make sure your site is fast and pages load in 2-3 seconds, tops!

- Technology/Devices - This lets you know what type of devices people are using to navigate your website, no matter if it's laptops, tablets, or smartphones. Additionally, they can let you know which Operating Systems people are using such as Windows, Android, iOS, Mac X, and more.

Next Level Websites

Now that we've looked at website basics, let's look at next level engagement. Websites are starting to incorporate Artificial Intelligence and Machine Learning. They are looking at our tendencies, viewing history, and how we have interacted with a website and creating websites that think for people. If we look at other major platforms like Google or Facebook, they tailor our online experiences based on data acquired from the internet about the user. So this is the model that many websites will begin to follow. They will tailor the website with content that is geared toward engaging them and their online experience. This is something that we can do on our websites as well. We can use cookies, web history, and other freely available information to develop a digital platform that creates a customized experience for every user, very similar to customized Google searches and customized social media newsfeeds based on AI and previous online habits.

So as you start to think about your present web experience, keep in mind this is what's coming, and by "what's coming" I mean it's already here.

CHAPTER 4 - MULTIMEDIA CONNECTIONS

Introduction

Multimedia is content that uses a combination of different content forms such as text, audio, images, animations, video and interactive content (Wikipedia). In this chapter we focus on the audio and video aspects of multimedia and how their use on certain platforms can help grow the online visibility of your organization. We will highlight YouTube, Internet TV, Podcasts and Internet Church Campuses (for our church readers), and how these platforms can be used in your digital strategy. There are many reasons to include multimedia in your digital strategy, below are a few to get you started.

Key Video Stats

- Videos under two minutes long get the most engagement. (Wistia)
- 85% of Facebook videos are watched without sound, while 60% of Instagram Stories are watched with the sound on. (Instagram)
- Google Chrome blocks autoplay ads as a way to make the 82% of consumers that hate autoplay stick around. (Marketing Land)
- 33% of viewers will stop watching a video after 30 seconds, 45% by one minute, and 60% by two minutes. (Ad Age)
- 93% of marketers use video. (SingleGrain)
- 73% of B2B marketers say video positively impacts their ROI. (Tubular Insights)
- 81% of businesses use video as a marketing tool — up from 63% over the last year. (Hubspot)
- Six out of 10 people would rather watch online videos than television. (Google)
- Mobile video consumption rises by 100% every year. (Insivia)

- By 2022, online videos will make up more than 82% of all consumer internet traffic — 15 times higher than it was in 2017. (Cisco)
- 78% of people watch online videos every week, and 55% view online videos every day. (HubSpot)
- YouTube is the second most popular website after Google. (Alexa)
- Users view more than 1 billion hours of video each day on YouTube. (YouTube)
- 59% of executives say they would rather watch a video than read text. (Wordstream)
- 75% of all video plays are on mobile devices. (eMarketer)
- Viewers retain 95% of a message when they watch it in a video, compared to 10% when reading it in text. (Insivia)
- 72% of customers would rather learn about a product or service by-way of video. (HubSpot)

- People are 1.5 times more likely to watch video on their mobile phones. (Facebook)
- 92% of users watching video on mobile will share it with others. (Wordstream)
- By 2020 there will be close to 1 million minutes of video crossing the internet per second. (Cisco)
- 65% of people use YouTube to help them solve a problem. Want to build a house or remove weird parasites from your eye? YouTube might have the answer. (Google)
- Social media posts with video have 48% more views. (HubSpot)
- 90% of Twitter video views happen on a mobile device. (Twitter)
- Over 1.9 billion people use YouTube. That's about one-third of the internet. (YouTube)
- 62% of people said they were more interested in a product after seeing it in a Facebook Story. (Marketing Land)

- Facebook has more than 8 billion video views-per-day. (TechCrunch)
- 75 million people visit Facebook's video platform every day. (Adweek)
- Social video generates 1200% more shares than text and image content combined. (G2 Crowd)
- Video promotions are now equally as popular as photo promotions on Facebook. (Socialbakers)
- Snapchat users watch 10 billion videos each day. (Mashable)
- Video campaigns on LinkedIn have 50% view rates. (LinkedIn)
- 81% of businesses prefer to use Facebook for their video marketing. (Buffer)
- Including a video on your landing page can boost your conversion rate by up to 80%. (Unbounce)
- Nearly 50% of internet users look for videos related to a product or service before visiting a store. (Hubspot)

- 25% of companies publish videos every week. (Buffer)
- 85% of consumers want to see more video content from brands. (HubSpot)
- 52% of marketers say video is the type of content with the best ROI (return on investment). (HubSpot)
- 50% of viewers aged 18-34 said they would stop what they were doing to watch a video from their favorite creators. (Google)
- On average, people spend 2.6x more time on pages with video than without. (Wistia)

YouTube is still on the Rise

YouTube has over one-billion views daily, with more than 300 hours of video uploaded every single-minute. Roughly half-of-the-views are via mobile devices, and the most dominant demographic group (millennials) swear by a YouTube video when they want to learn more about anything, find a review, or enjoy some form of entertainment, easily and for free.

Everyone from individuals and small-businesses-to-organizations and global corporations, need to include video in their digital marketing strategies. While figuring out how to integrate it varies widely by your goal and mission, simply having video content guarantees your audience will use it.

Video is more engaging, but also a preferred consumer medium. One-minute of video, according to some researchers, is worth roughly 1.8 million printed words of marketing language. And it no longer takes a degree in film studies and technology to create good content that you can make available online.

The world has seen so many videos become viral, and we all know that there is no formula that can ensure something explodes across the web. However, there is one-thing that can maximize the reach, and that is the use of YouTube for your content.

The site currently makes it remarkably easy for account holders to post their videos, tag them heavily with the best keywords, give them titles and descriptions that work in favor of SEO, and Google natively includes the site's videos in any search results. The ability to easily share to such social media as Facebook, Twitter, and a score of other sites, embed it into a website, or share via email, ensures that a well-made video gets maximum mileage. The mobility of the site, which is easily used on any tablet or phone, also increases its viability as a major marketing channel and tool.

If you are looking for a single site to leverage your marketing energy, it is to YouTube where you should turn your attention. The site has grown tremendously, and is not showing any signs of slowing down. In fact, it seems to be increasing over time. Your audience may not say it, but they prefer video content, and it is important to be sure that it is a major element in your marketing plan. If you have not yet explored this opportunity, today is the day to-do-so.

YouTube Strategies

When developing your YouTube strategy, it's best to take a multi-step approach. Always remember, YouTube is owned by Google, and is the second largest search engine on the internet. YouTube is a video platform first and foremost, but that is not all that it is. It's a place where people search for video based solutions for issues, inspiration and education. Once your video is ready, then comes the next steps listed below:

1. Create Great Content - It's important that you develop great video content that is YouTube ready. Every video you post does not have to be a professional production, but for videos that you want significant engagement, make sure they are filmed with great cameras, have quality audio and are edited to look great.

2. Do More than Just Post Videos - Now this is the key part, DO NOT JUST POST VIDEOS AND HOPE PEOPLE FIND THEM. You have to put in the effort and work to make that video visible and easy to find for people that are looking for that content. Therefore, once you have uploaded your video, now the real work

begins. Now you need to fill out the content categories and setup this video to be as highly visible as possible.

3. Fill out the Title and Descriptions - The title and description of the video are very important to getting your video discovered. Make sure the title and description both include keywords that can help people find your videos. Take time to think through your video description so that it accurately describes your video and also gives key links that you may want your viewers to use after watching the video. Links could include your homepage, online store, key people in the video, social media and other aspects of the video that have external links.

4. Add Tags and Hashtags - The tags section is one of the key ways that YouTube organizes videos on its platform. This is the section where you can take the premise of your video and break it down into a number of keywords that you can put in this section. Additionally, YouTube has now allowed you to add hashtags to the "top line" -- when users search for those keywords, hashtags will come up as well. It's a great addition by YouTube to include the hashtag feature.

5. Create Playlists and Build out Channel Page - When users come to your page and you have numerous, unorganized videos, it can be difficult for them to efficiently find the videos they are searching for. It can also be difficult for your church to guide them through your videos and help them see the wealth of video

content your YouTube channel has to offer. Therefore, Playlists are a great organizational tool to help categorize your videos into topical collections. Playlists also allow users to see all of your channel's videos organized in chronological order, giving them an easier way to view the content. When you are logged into your YouTube page, you want to go to the "Creator Studio," click on the "Dashboard" on the top left, and finally click on the "View Channel" option so that you can build the look and feel of your channel. Make sure to update your YouTube channel art (header) so that, no matter what device you are watching, your channel looks amazing. YouTube recommends uploading channel art at 2560 x 1440 px with a max file size of 2MB. Next, make sure to create a featured video that will show when people who aren't subscribers visit your channel. Lastly, you want to add your Social Media icons and links to your YouTube page so subscribers can connect with you on other platforms. I also recommend that you put your official website link on your YouTube page.

6. YouTube Cards and Boxes - While viewers are watching, guide them where you want them to go. YouTube provides are few tools to do this such as cards and boxes. YouTube Cards are calls-to-action within the video. When you are watching YouTube videos, the links, subscribes, bubbles, pop-ups, or anything clickable you see that causes an action within the video is a Card. When you get to the end of the video and they ask you do you want to view another video or subscribe, those are YouTube boxes. You set each of these features up in the

editing section of your video, which allow you to give your users quite a few options of what to do while watching your videos.

Internet TV

The traditional (analog) TV industry is being disrupted and fighting for dear life. The traditional content producers (studios) and the cable companies held on to that old business model till the last dollar was squeezed out of it, but now, the market is starting to dictate how things will play out and just as the music industry was made to adapt, the television industry will have the same fate.

We already see this happening with television viewing going from analog delivery to digital media. We are more immersed in social media connected viewing along with second screens, and we watch what we want to watch, when we want to watch and from any device we want to watch. No more cable bundles and set showtimes. A la carte channels, not bundles, are becoming how we choose our channels, which is vastly different from our current cable company offerings.

Currently, Internet television devices such as the Roku, Google ChromeCast, Amazon Fire TV and Apple TV are just getting started in changing our living room experience. These devices and the platforms that support them are significantly smarter than traditional TV's. These devices know our watching habits, how long we watch, what we talk about during shows as well as our demographics. This will be a goldmine for these platforms as their recommendations will get better and we will watch more. Advertisers will want to be on these platforms based on this in-depth viewing information. This is what will drive innovation... the advertising dollars. That is the final piece in helping the content producing studios (and even cable companies) in moving to this future television experience because now the financial benefits are realized.

Organizations have an opportunity like no other today to reach people who watch television. Previously, it could cost upwards of $50,000 per week to run on traditional television stations and you didn't even have the tools to fully analyze your viewing audience. With the Internet TV platforms that we have today, a company can get started for as little as FREE (instanttvchannel.com) and have a channel setup in an hour. Your organization can now get on Internet TV enabled devices such as Roku, Apple TV or Amazon Fire for affordable pricing and setup a TV app for your company that can reach millions.

When you setup your channel, there are two main delivery channel formats, one is the on-demand format where you upload videos and categorize them according to topics and let people choose what they want to watch. Another is a running channel that continuously broadcasts shows 24/7. Therefore, whenever someone comes to the channel they can view continuous programming. You should run your internet channel like a real television station, with pre-rolls, lower thirds, post-rolls, on-screen hashtags for social interaction and other ways we see traditional tv channels engage their viewing audience.

Internet TV is the future and everyday we get closer to that reality. Every major cable network has a streaming only Internet TV option in addition to Hulu, YouTube and Sling having live TV options. Cord cutters are becoming the norm and younger viewers are bypassing live TV all together and just subscribing to services like Hulu, Netflix and Amazon Prime for their viewing needs. With the current generation becoming cord cutters, the next generation bypassing cable and the youngest generation watching YouTube only, traditional TV's viewing model is on a countdown.

Podcasts

Podcast is a term that is entering the common vocabulary in the same way that Google and other computer specific terminology have done in the past few years. In the past, a podcast was an oddity that belonged exclusively to those who owned the iPod (the term is built from combining "broadcasting" and iPod after all). Today, podcasts can be streamed through a web browser, music streaming platforms, podcast apps through a RSS subscription, or loaded to any device capable of interacting with the Internet.

There are a few technical terms that anyone interested in making podcasts should know, and among them is the new definition of a podcast. For all intents and purposes,

they are digital files that are made to be downloaded to a computer or media player. They can be "one-off" episodes, but are most often a series of recordings about a subject or specific area of interest.
So, they are not limited to the iPod owners, and they are not exactly broadcasts. They are what you should refer to as "content syndication". Though you can use places like iTunes and Google Play to find podcasts, you can also subscribe to your favorites (via their websites as well as online stores) and have them delivered to you directly, however you choose to receive it.

Why You Should Be Making Podcasts

Okay, so that is the technical description of the podcast, and now it is time to look at precisely why you want or need one. After all, you may be like so many others in the modern world and have already written a blog or you used social media to promote ideas or your business, and even maintained a website. Why add yet another item to the "to-do" list?

Reasonably, there is no single, easy answer. Instead, there is a list of really great reasons that you need to roll up your sleeves, clear your throat, and start talking:

- They are hot and have become one of the most popular ways for people to generate content. Take the tremendous success of something like Serial and the offshoots it has created to see just how effective a well-made podcast can be.

- They are a potent form of content unlike anything else in the list of possibilities. After all, blogs, videos, social media, articles, websites... they don't exactly travel well. They can connect us to an idea, but that connection breaks when we walk away from the computer. Podcasts come with us on any media player and people often talk about taking them into the shower, out on the road, on walks, as they do chores, and more. Content is king, and podcasts are a way of bringing that content out into the world in the most dynamic way imaginable.

- They speak to us. Yes, they are recordings that are speaking, but have you ever had to read a sentence twice because the meaning was unclear? The spoken word doesn't run that risk. When podcasting, your message is spoken clearly, with emotion, and even with inflection at just the right points.

- Podcasts can be transcribed into dynamic written content and used for posting to a blog, website or social media, and all without running the risk of taking some hits to SEO results.

- They are ideal conduits for guest content, and it is much more likely that you can get a 15-minute phone call with your guests, than that 500-1000 word article that tends to be "guest content".

- They are so easy-to-make. Go ahead and record a podcast and then try to achieve the same sort of content goals with writing. Record, edit, and release is all that it takes, and then it is up-to-you to promote it.

And now that you know the reasons for making podcasts, it's time to consider how to get your podcast uploaded, so you can build an audience around them.

Apple iTunes and Google Play Music in Addition to Your Sites

The places that people can listen to podcasts include the actual website with its RSS feed, or they can subscribe to the podcast by uploading it via iTunes or Google Play Music. Thus, you want your podcasts to appear on these venues. To do this takes one thing: Following instructions.

Both iTunes and Google Play Music have very specific guidelines that you must follow if your podcast is accepted and then placed in the store. While it is possible for us to give you the instructions here, it would be better for you to use the very latest versions from the sources themselves:

- Apple - http://www.apple.com/itunes/podcasts/specs.html
- Google - https://g.co/podcastportal

Something to note about using both sites is that there are tips and suggestions available for increasing your chances at success. For example, Apple provides a long list of tips for "Creating Podcast Feeds and Metadata" that you just cannot ignore. These suggestions include taking advantage of tagging, using strong subcategories, and choosing a strong title. Why? So you can be found by an audience looking for your kind of content.

Remember that neither Google Play Music nor Apple iTunes sites can work with you unless you have your RSS feed up and running, and Google Play Music strongly suggests using the same RSS feed link that you submitted to iTunes. Naturally, a high quality show, good visuals and sound, and effective music and content must enter the equation too.

By now, you know that a podcast is becoming an essential part of any content marketing plan, and it is a far more dynamic and unusual way to spread your message.

Internet Church Campuses

Church is happening outside the walls of the sanctuary, and churches need to adapt and take the ministry to the people. Additionally, the way people want to connect with their churches has expanded beyond the traditional midweek and weekend services. Now they want to connect 24 hours a day, seven-days-a-week, from anywhere in the world on any Internet-enabled device.

Enter the Internet church campus and the need for an online extension of the offline church. The Internet church campus is more than a streaming page that broadcasts live services a few times a week. It's a fully functional, interactive online experience with an online pastor and online members.

This is not just a place for people who don't want to come to service and choose to watch online—this is a place for people who are online members of this church and possibly live in places where traditional church locations are not an option. Here are the five ways to make your online church experience better.

<u>Establish Key Goals for Your Online Church Experience</u>

As with any church initiative, you need to have a strategy with goals. When it comes to establishing goals for your online church experience, here are some key questions to ask yourself:

- Do you mimic the offline church experience in the online space or just create a streaming channel?
- Who will lead the initiative? The person who set it up or will you have an online pastor?

If you are looking to create an online church then you should take a look at your offline church experience and see what you can duplicate in the online space. You don't have to start out with a full online church experience, but that should be your goal... to build an online community with your online church. When you are looking to choose who will lead this online church, consider the same thought process when you choose a men's ministry leader or a women's ministry leader. The person who leads the online ministry experience should be just as experienced and willing to learn about the online space as the person who leads the men's ministry or women's ministry is experienced in their area.

Choose a Great Platform

This is just as important as choosing your church building and location. There isn't a better option out there than Church Online Platform - https://churchonlineplatform.com/. This platform is free and gives you options such as scheduling (one-time and repeating), chat, giving, branding and live or simulated services. This is the best platform to start, engage and grow your online church community.

Will Your Ministry Show Live Services or Simulated?

Notice that the question was not "which one was better," because that is not the most important question, in my opinion. When you look at the capabilities of the ministry in terms of cameras, internet speed within the sanctuary and the technical expertise of the camera/production crew, then it becomes more evident on which type of service your ministry should do. If your ministry has the capability to put on a high quality live service, then by all means do so. On the other hand, if it is easier to just record the service and then edit the video and show it later on, then do that. Don't sacrifice quality for speed, or just being able to say you are streaming live.

Establish Goals for the People Watching

This is where the rubber meets the road in taking your online church from just a "way to watch services" to a "full online church community experience". You have to establish goals and ways to integrate the online viewers into full online members of the church, the same way you have ways to take new visitors to your church and integrate them into your church membership. Here are some key questions to answer as you are creating this online church experience.

- How will you help them get saved?
  Once an online viewer mentions that they want to be saved, many churches have a page they direct them to where they can watch as the online pastor guides them through the prayer of salvation. Once that is complete, then they make sure they stay connected as they embark on their new spiritual journey.

- How will you integrate them into the church?
  You can create this by giving them online forms to fill out during or after the online service, so that you can capture key information to stay connected with

them. Also, once they have decided to become a part of your online church, you need to have ways for them to become online members, learn more about what it means to be a christian and a part of your church online, as well as ways for them to give donations (I'll discuss this in more detail later) and ways to get plugged into the online community and start to serve.

- How will you help them in their continued walk of faith?
  Many churches use lifegroups to help their members in their continued spiritual development and walk of faith. If you have life groups offline, how will you create them online and integrate them into it. Facebook groups are a great way to set up groups that you can guide online members to. This is where you can communicate with them weekly and help them in their spiritual walk as well as give them a place to communicate and fellowship with others.

<u>Acknowledge the online church viewers from the pulpit</u>

As your ministry transitions from seeing the online church as "just a place to stream services" to an "online community of worshippers", then you will understand how important it is to acknowledge them from the pulpit. The Ministry interacts with the people offline in the sanctuary therefore there is no reason not to interact with the ones online in the virtual sanctuary. Convince leadership to not get stuck in the tradition of routine services where you only speak to the church members you can see as if those are the only ones that need a Word.

Examples of Great Online Churches

- Saddleback Online Campus - https://saddleback.com/visit/locations/onlinecampus
- LifeChurch - https://live.life.church/
- The Worship Center - https://theworshipcentercc.churchonline.org/

CHAPTER 5 - ECOMMERCE CONNECTIONS

Introduction

In 2019 there will be an estimated 1.92 billion people (25% of the 7.7 billion global population) who use the internet for ecommerce, that's a lot of potential customers/donors. This number is rising rapidly and expected to hit 2.1 billion by 2021 (Oberlo). Here are some key eCommerce stats:

- 30% of online giving occurs in December. 10% on the last three days of the year. (NonProfit Source)

- In 2017, 21% of online donations were made on a mobile device (Charitable Giving Report)

- The number one reason people shop online is that they're able to shop at all hours of the day. (Oberlo)
- Nearly 40% of all online purchases made during the 2018 holiday season were done on smartphones. (Outerbox)
- 80% of Americans are online shoppers. More than half of them have made purchases on mobile devices. (Pew Research Center)
- People who have a bad mobile experience with your business are 62% less likely to become your customer in the future. (Google)
- 69% of smartphone users say they're more likely to buy from businesses with mobile sites or apps that answer their questions. (Google)
- 59% of smartphone users favor businesses with mobile sites or apps that enable them to make purchases easily and quickly. (Think with Google)
- 85% of consumers conduct online research before making a purchase online. (Oberlo)

- 65% of shoppers look-up price comparisons on their mobile device while in a physical store. (Oberlo)

- 81% of consumers trust the advice of friends and family over businesses. (Hubspot)

- 80% of people stop doing business with a company because of poor customer experience(s). (Oberlo)

- 69% of shopping carts are abandoned. (Oberlo)

- On average, 52% of online stores have omnichannel capabilities. (Oberlo)

Make it Easy

Amazon has a normal checkout which is 2-3 steps or they have a one-step checkout. The 2-3 step checkout is to check your transaction, make sure it's correct, register your information/shipping and then checkout, which is not an issue for most people. Likewise, the one-step checkout is for people who want to log-in, complete their transaction and keep it moving, that's the definition of easy. When you create eCommerce processes for your organization, make sure that your online giving (website, sms, app, etc.) follows this model. Many people do not give online due to the process taking too long and/or having too many steps.

Make it Secure

Every year we hear of a major hack that occurs with a major corporation. Most recently it was Capital One, Equifax and Experian. Interestingly enough, while consumer trust didn't increase or decrease, it did shed a light on the lack of security that many organizations have online. While no website/online system is hack-proof, there are steps you can take to make sure your online donation process is secure and encrypted. First, you need to get a SSL (Secure Socket Layer) certificate with at least 128-bit encryption for your online donation page. This certificate, which can be purchased from Godaddy.com or Verisign.com changes your web address from http://www.domainname.com to https://www.domainname.com (note the http changing to https which means the website transaction is secure during the payment process). Once this certificate is purchased and installed on your website server, your online transactions are much more secure.

Make It Accessible

In case you missed the mobile stats above, I will reiterate here. Nearly 40% of all online purchases made during the 2018 holiday season were done on smartphones. Eighty-percent of Americans are online shoppers. More than half-of-them have made purchases on mobile devices. Fifty-nine percent of smartphone users favor businesses with mobile sites or apps that enable them to make purchases easily and quickly. People who have a bad mobile experience with your business are 62% less likely to become your customer in the future. Sixty-nine percent of smartphone users say they're more likely to buy from businesses with mobile sites or apps that answer their questions. These key mobile statistics highlight the importance of a mobile online giving and mobile shopping experience.

Additionally, with the rise in popularity of Apple Pay and Google Pay, which allow purchases to be made in stores, online and in apps right from your phone, the mobile payment process is becoming even easier. Oh, I almost forgot, when you add in Venmo and Cash App, we are seeing the use of mobile to quickly send and receive money from others. These mobile-based financial behaviors are continuing to grow, and it's not just a young mobile user thing. One of the most used financial apps, Cash App, has been growing amongst parents and grandparents who want to send money to their children and grandchildren. Therefore, as these apps become more commonplace for younger users, they will continue to grow well into the future. Each of these apps can play a significant role in your eCommerce strategy.

Online Giving

In my past books, I have dedicated a section to online giving and talked about ways to set up online giving in your digital strategy. I will discuss that only briefly because I want to focus on a different aspect of online giving in this book. When it comes to online giving solutions, make sure you have a full solution like Pushpay.com, Titlhe.ly or

RebelGive from ProChurchTools.com. However, if you decide you want to create your own giving form and do things yourself, then you can use Jotform.com and integrate a Stripe.com or Paypal.com account to connect with your bank and just take online donations that way.

Now, let's look at another aspect when it comes to online giving methods, one-time givers versus recurring givers. The goal is to make it easy for both options. Many times I have seen online donation sites, especially with churches, focus on recurring givers and thus make the one-time giving process more difficult. Additionally, I have seen sites, where they only focus on one-time givers and don't give users the tools to setup recurring giving. My suggestion is to provide both with easy solutions. If you have a full service provider like we discussed before, then make sure they give users a way to login and give (recurring) or just give as a guest (one-time). This gives the user the option to choose how to support the ministry and makes it EASY to do so.

Why the Amazon Shopping Experience Is so Easy

When you are looking for something you need to buy, is your first instinct to head to Amazon to see what the site has available? If so, you certainly aren't alone. Over the years, Amazon has grown from a bookseller into an online retail powerhouse. The experience of buying through Amazon has become better and more streamlined, as well.

The Site Is Easy to Use

Amazon has a website that is easy to use with all of the information that a potential buyer needs right at their fingertips. It is easy to search for any item that you might need, and you can easily add and remove items from your cart. You can also add wish lists of items that you want and you can look at wish lists of people you know, to see what they might want for a gift. Amazon thinks about what will make the customer's life easier as they are shopping and continues to make improvements to streamline the online buying process, such as their "1-click" buying option.

They Have the Products You Want at Good Prices

Amazon might have started out focusing on books, but they can provide customers with just about anything they may be interested in purchasing. Not only do they have a lot of products, they often have products from sellers that are competing. This means that Amazon and the sellers they work with tend to offer very low prices, making it cheaper to buy through them than a store in your area, even when you consider shipping costs.

It Is Personalized

Amazon can also provide personalized service. They know what you buy and have bought, and they can make recommendations for similar products. The personalized service can make it easier for people to find other items that they might not even have known they wanted or needed.

Good Customer Service

Amazon has worked hard to develop a responsive and helpful customer service team that can easily be accessed online and on the phone. This is not to say that they never make missteps, but overall, people tend to have a positive experience when they deal with Amazon's customer service team.

Fast Shipping

Today, people have a mindset where they want the items that they order as soon as possible. They want it the same day or the next day in many cases, and Amazon's shipping options and policies make this possible. It wasn't too many years ago that placing an order through the mail or online would mean a week or several weeks of waiting. That's not the case any longer.

These are just some of the reasons that Amazon has become as popular as it has and the reason it is often the first place that people consider looking when they are shopping. Even if there might be a store in the area that they could visit, many people simply love the convenience that Amazon offers and will order through them. Other companies that want to do better with their customers will want to look at the places where Amazon succeeds and see if they might be able to emulate them.

What This Means For Your Organization

When you decide you want to create an online store, Amazon is the gold standard that you want to follow. Each of the key areas we described above make the Amazon experience one of the best. Now, when it comes to organizations like yours who want to match this experience, there are software platforms like Shopify.com to help you create a great online store experience for your customers. But keep in mind, Amazon isn't just an eCommerce platform, there are many people that help with customer support, shipping and other areas that make it so much more. So keep that in mind when you are creating your online experience.

New eCommerce Models

Now that we've talked about current eCommerce models, let's focus on what's coming down the line. When I think about the future of eCommerce, I think of cryptocurrency. Crypto, as it's called for short, is a mystery to many people because it encompasses not just the actual currency but also the way that it is distributed and stored. Cryptocurrency is defined as a digital currency in which encryption techniques are used to regulate the generation of units of currency and verify the transfer of funds, operating independently of a central bank. Many people think of bitcoin when they think of cryptocurrency and while bitcoin is the most popular one, it's not the only one. There are a variety of other altcoins such as Ripple, Litecoin, Tron, Ethereum and many more. These coins all symbolize a form of cryptocurrency and an underlying technology that supports them known as blockchain. Blockchain is defined as a system in which a record of transactions made in bitcoin or another cryptocurrency are maintained across several computers that are linked in a peer-to-peer network.

Since crypto operates outside of a central bank, the value of it fluctuates compared to a traditional currency like the American dollar. The true value in crypto is in the amount of goods and services you can exchange it for in the online space. Therefore, in these early days, crypto does not provide much value and it's unstable valuation makes it a risky investment. However, as time progresses and crypto's value stabilizes and its usage becomes less of a fringe thing, then it's value will increase.

One of the best ways to purchase cryptocurrency is on Coinbase.com in the United States and Binance.com if you are outside the US. The benefits of these online exchanges is that you can take fiat currency (American dollars) and exchange them for crypto. This is the easiest way to get started in using crypto if you are interested. One of the key books that I read recently that talks about ways to use crypto for nonprofits was by my good friend Nils Smith. This book, co-written by Nick Runyon is called *Crypto for Good* and it's on Amazon. It delves into many ways that nonprofits can use crypto to support their missions and get ahead of the curve.

CHAPTER 6 - SOCIAL MEDIA CONNECTIONS

What's New in Social

Social media has changed the way we live our lives. From the way we get our news, the way we share stories and the way we interact with our loved ones. Social media is everywhere. It's unavoidable, it's powerful, and it's here to stay. Social media usage continues to grow every year and it continues to become an integral part of everyday life. It continues to unify us in ways that we never imagined, likewise it continues to divide us irreparably. Some of the keys to social media these days are catered content, micro-storytelling, engagement, customer service, social commerce and echo-chambers. While these are not all the key areas of impact, they are some of the most important. As we look at some of these key areas of social media in this chapter, keep in mind that social media continues to evolve rapidly and it will continue to be an important aspect of every part of our lives.

Key stats

- 3.4 billion social media users (WeArSocial)
- An average of 142 minutes is spent on social media everyday (Oberlo)
- 2.4 billion monthly Facebook users (Facebook)
- 1.9 billion monthly YouTube users (Google)
- 1.5 billion monthly WhatsApp users (Goodfirms.co)
- 1 billion monthly Instagram users (Facebook)
- 326 million monthly Twitter users (Twitter)
- 260 million monthly Linkedin users (Linkedin)
- 300 million monthly Snapchat users (Snapchat)
- 6000 tweets are sent per second (InternetLiveStats)
- 1 million Facebook links are shared every 20 minutes (InternetLiveStats)
- Instagram has 500 million daily active stories (Oberlo)
- 91% of social media users access channels via mobile devices (Oberlo)

Micro-storytelling

What is one of the best ways to let people know more about yourself, your brand, and your products? As always, you need a good story and you need to have a way to tell it well. Stories have always been important to people, and even though the way we consume stories have changed since we were huddled in caves and telling tales around campfires. The power and importance of storytelling has never dwindled.

In fact, stories have been used in branding and marketing for a number of years in different ways. Companies have used stories to help their customers see beyond the business aspect and instead see into the people of the company and what makes it tick. Today, there are social media features that encourage various types of storytelling for many purposes.

Stories Need to Be Compelling

Boring stories that do not provide information or entertainment of some sort are not going to make people want to take action.They will not want to learn more about you, your company, or your product. Find a way to make what you have to say compelling and interesting – instead of just trying to push a product.

Stories Need to Be Short

Because of the nature of social media, you will also need to keep the stories short. The length may vary based on the platform, but the shorter the better. Only use as much time/space as you need to tell the story.

Stories Need to Have Structure and a Call-to-Action

A good story will have a beginning, a middle, and an end. They need to reach some sort of satisfying conclusion, or they need to indicate that there is more to the story that you will tell somewhere else. This is where you could put in a call-to-action, for example, having people learn more on your site. The call-to-action can be simple, such as asking people to follow you or share the story. Regardless of your methods, there should always be a call-to-action option available.

Place Stories on the Right Apps/Sites

Understanding how to create stories that work is very important. However, you also need to make sure that you are using the right app for your stories. Think about which of the apps your customers, or people you want to be customers, are most likely to use. That should be your primary focus, but you can and should attempt to use the other apps as well, to see what types of results they can bring.

Quality Over Quantity: Benefits of Engagement in Social Media Over Numbers

There is still an old mindset of "more is better" that many people believe, and some believe that it applies to all aspects of the business. They feel that more product is better, more ads are better, more followers are better, and they believe that all of this will equate to more success and more money. However, the math of more does not always add up. Sometimes, spending more on advertising and trying to gain as many followers as possible means you are gaining low-quality followers who do not really care about your company. You could be losing money and not making the most of your social media.

Who Are the Right Followers?

It tends to be a much better option to make sure you are trying to find the right followers and fans on social media rather than just trying to get as many as possible. When you have a smaller group of people who actually care about who you are, what you have to say, and what you are offering, you will find that the results are better all-around.

Not only will social media feel more productive for you, but it will also yield better results. After all, if you have 100,000 people following you and most of them do not care about the products you make, you won't get many sales. If you have 2,000 followers who use and understand the types of products you make or services you offer, you are already more likely to make sales.

When you actually take the time to engage with that audience and show them that there are real people behind the company who care about them and their needs, things can get even better for you. This can help to breed brand loyalty. They become ambassadors for your brand by telling their friends and family about you, and by spreading the word online through social media sites.

Engaging with the Audience

Social media is supposed to be social, so be sure that you are communicating with and interacting with the followers you have. The increased interaction is good for developing a rapport. You can ask questions, make comments, host a Q&A, and more. When you engage, it not only helps to promote brand loyalty, but it can also help you to get more people to your website.

People have come to expect responses on social media when they have questions and concerns. Most companies have learned that it is important to respond in a relatively quick manner, as well, or else it can look like the company is ignoring their customers. In fact, many people today will go through social media for customer service before they will contact the actual customer service department.

Social media can also become a good tool to learn more about customers and what they really want and expect. All of this information can help to guide your company in the future.

The Rise of Stories on Facebook and Instagram

Visual content has always been important, whether it is in marketing or providing information and entertainment for an audience. It's why movies and television became as popular as they are, and it's why sites online that provide visual content are as successful as they are. People love stories, whether they are the ones telling them or they are the ones listening to them. Technology has made it easier than ever to consume stories.

Mobile Has Helped with the Rise of Social Media Stories

People today have smartphones, which means they can quickly and easily access the Internet and have an experience very similar to if they were on a desktop or laptop. They use their phones to get access to social media sites like Instagram and Facebook, and they enjoy the stories that are being added there. In fact, there are hundreds of millions of stories posted to these sites daily from all across the world.

Many of them are added by users who want to share what's happening in their life. However, quite a few companies have followed suit as well, and they are adding stories to help get the word out about their company and their products.

Regardless of why people are posting stories, they are being viewed in large numbers by a worldwide audience. The use of these technologies has made it much easier for people all around the world to communicate and share stories with one another. It has also made it easier for businesses, nonprofits, and more to share their own stories with the world.

Different People and Different Brands Naturally Tell Different Stories

While there are some basics that people will want to keep in mind when it comes to creating a good story, the stories told will vary greatly. The types of stories and the posting strategies will need to depend on the personality or the brand that is telling them.

They can be a great way to show off events that are occurring, they can be used for glimpses behind the scenes, they can help to show off a product, and more. For the best results, no matter who is posting a story, the story should be compelling and it should have a beginning middle and end just like any story. It does not matter that it's short and online in a video format.

People Enjoy These Types of Stories

The audiovisual formats of these stories on Facebook and Instagram have captured the attention of countless millions of people who are using these sites. There is an audience out there for you no matter how cliché you might think it will be. When you use the stories features on these sites, it can help you to grow the number of followers you have, increase your social media presence, and in the case of businesses, it can help to provide more sales. Just make sure you understand the ins and outs of the platforms that you will be using.

Pay-to-Play: The Power of Paid Ads on Social Media

There is a saying that goes, in order to make money, you have to spend money. While the Internet has helped to level the playing field between many businesses, there is still some truth to this statement. Having paid ads on social media, for example, has the potential to expose your brand and products to people faster and much easier than through organic advertising only done on your website.

Go Where the People Are

It has always been true that you want to advertise where there are people to see the ads. This is why people and companies in the past would target their ads to newspapers, TV, and radio. At the time, that was the best place to reach large numbers of people. However, this approach was often like throwing everything at the wall to see what stuck. It was difficult to target a niché audience, even with TV when you could choose the programs where the ads were run. It also happened to be quite expensive.

Social media and the Internet have helped to change things for the better for marketers.

Instead of using a scattershot approach, which was typically expensive and not always effective, marketers today have a better handle on the demographics of their audience. Thanks to social media, they are also able to target their specific audience when they are using the paid marketing services. This means that the ads are being put in front of people who might actually appreciate them and who will be more likely to take action.

The action they take will depend on the nature of the ad, of course. You might request that they follow you, click-to-head to your website, sign-up for a newsletter, or make an actual purchase.

With social media sites, such as Facebook, you can target your ad specifically toward the ideal demographic for your business. You can choose the age, location, gender, interests, and more, meaning that your ad will show up for people who fall into that category. Even if they do not click on the ad now, they become more accustomed to seeing your name and brand. Over time, it can build trust.

A Cost-Effective Option

Because you will have more control over who is seeing the advertisements, it means that you are spending your marketing dollars wisely. This tends to provide you with much better performance for your ads. Paid ads through social media can work just as well for B2B (business-to-business) as it can for B2C (business-to-customer).

Easy to Measure

Social media paid ads are also easy to measure in terms of their reach and their success. This will let you know relatively quickly whether an ad is working or whether you need to make some changes to it.

If you want to make the most of online ads, make it a point to invest some of your marketing budgets into social media advertisements. It can help you to reach customers that you might not have found elsewhere.

Analytics

Social media analytics give every organization the opportunity to understand quite a few things when it comes to their online audience. First, it gives organizations a glimpse into how their online audience is engaging with them. Secondly, it gives them insight into how their competitors are using social media platforms. Lastly, it helps organizations to analyze, optimize and repeat their social media strategy so that it can become a better engagement and marketing channel for the business.

When it comes to analyzing an organization's online audience, the analytics should focus on engagement and not just numbers. We highlighted earlier on how quality (engagement) is better than quantity (numbers), therefore when looking at the analytics of social media channels, let the engagement guide the strategy. Social media has evolved into an industry that is best utilized when engagement is the priority. Therefore, 1000 highly-engaged fans are better than 100,000 followers who rarely speak.

Social media provides great insight into your competitors by allowing you to see their strategies and tactics when it comes to marketing their products and services online. Also, you can see how they tie their social presence into their other digital properties and thus adapt and adjust your social media presence accordingly.

CHAPTER 7 - MOBILE CONNECTIONS

The advent of smartphones means we are connected at all times and can easily find answers to our most obscure questions. Now-a-days we can order a pizza through one small device. In fact, mobile has taken over to such an extent that the following statistics are now true:

- 62% of users accessed the internet using their mobile phones. (Statista)
- By 2020, the number of smartphone users is projected to reach 2.87 billion. (Statista)
- Global: In November 2018, Statista measured that, mobile devices accounted for 48.2% of website traffic worldwide - excluding tablets. (Statista)

- 50% of smartphone owners now check mobile devices, first thing in the morning. (Omnicore)
- On average, 23 Billion SMS messages were sent daily in 2018. (Smseagle)
- Consumers spending hit $930 Billion USD, using mobile payment applications. (Upwork)
- China had the highest number of smartphone users in 2018: 775 million. (NewZoo)
- United Kingdom had the highest number for smartphone penetration: 82.2% or 54 million smartphone users out of 66 million population. Followed by the Netherlands with 80% and Sweden by 79%. (NewZoo)
- Average smartphone users used their phones for more than 4 hours a day. (Themanifest)
- 1/5 or 20% of millennials open an app at least 50 times a day. (Themanifest)
- 71% of teenagers watch an average of over 3 hours of videos online daily. (Thinkwithgoogle)

- 78% of teenagers now have access to a smartphone. (Thinkwithgoogle)
- Most 13-17 year olds, as of 2018, got their first smartphone at an earlier age of only 13. (Thinkwithgoogle)
- 52% of all teens now use at least one messaging app. (Thinkwithgoogle)
- 51% of all teens use at least one social networking app. (Thinkwithgoogle)
- 70% of all teens regularly make purchases online. (Thinkwithgoogle)
- 39%, most frequently used apps are of social media category. (Themanifest)
- 55% of social media engagement is on a mobile device. (Hubspot)
- 82% of customers use their mobile phone while making a decision about purchasing in-store. (Omnicore)
- 46% of people read reviews of all purchases on their mobile phones. (LinkedIn)
- 62% of people use their mobiles for price comparison. (LinkedIn)

- Mobile-influenced offline spending was more than $1 Trillion. (Biznessapps)
- In 2018, mobile commerce sales were over $626 billion. (Smartinsights)
- 69% of digital media time is spent on mobile devices. (Comscore)
- Google-owned 95% of the market of all US paid search on mobiles. (SearchEnginсLand)
- 40% of all mobile searches are for a local business or interest. (Omnicore)

The numbers just keep coming, with all of them pointing to some very obvious truths. The key factor among them is that any marketing plan for any organization must recognize the ways in which mobile has had an effect on marketing.

Think Mobile First...Right?

When we hear about digital strategies, we always hear people say “Think Mobile First”. This perspective is quite understandable and I find it to be very true, but not the whole truth. Thinking mobile first helps us, because according to Comscore.com, there are more mobile-only users than desktop only users. Google has also said that as of March

2015 there are more searches on mobile than on desktop. Therefore, when you want to connect with the growing digital audience of over 3 billion internet users, with 2 billion of them being mobile, you should think mobile first. The caveat in all of this is, what's driving this explosive mobile growth?

There are many factors that are leading the growth in mobile, which includes more than 6 billion mobile devices, over 4 million mobile apps and the growth of SMS/Texting. But above all of those factors, lies one major reason and that is social media. Social media has exploded due to mobile and mobile has exploded due to social media. Social media has undeniably transformed the way we use the internet and it has surpassed email as our main form of communication. Additionally, we have seen social media quickly become the top usage on mobile devices based on which top apps are downloaded when someone receives a new mobile device.

The focus here is not one to rehash the reasons why you should add social media to your digital strategy. I believe that's understood by the majority of organizations. The focus is also not to convince organizations to understand the importance of mobile. That's understood by organizations as they look at their employees and audience and see how many of them have mobile devices. This focus here is to help you understand how important mobile and social are together, as foundations for digital strategies to take your message to the masses. When you think about a digital strategy, consider that the majority of people will read your content and connect with your organization online from a mobile device as well as they will connect with, share and discuss this content and your organization via social media. Mobile and social go hand-in-hand and it would benefit our organizations to make strategies that highlight this trend.

As Mobile Evolves

"Our dependency on mobile devices for information has forced the design of the web to change. Netizens have come to expect mobile content is optimized in a way that brings them exactly what they are looking for front and center." (Techcrunch)

This is one of the key reasons for the development of "cards". This is actually a technology that "collapses online content into digital containers for fast and easy consumption … they are shortcuts designed to fill immediate needs, saving time and providing information in an easily digestible format while keeping people engaged where they are." (Techcrunch) A prime example of this is found by typing in the word "weather" at the Google site and enjoying a "card" that gives you the current information for your location (if you have allowed that on your mobile device or PC).

Streamlined, uncomplicated, and requiring little effort, cards organize multiple items into "stacks" and allow easy scrolling and single click activation of a card to expand its content. Rather than scrolling through a list of links, leading to a loss of engagement, the cards bring everything into easy focus.

Interestingly enough, the use of cards for mobile display has led to a startling result: "Consumer behavior has shifted from wanting apps to wanting answers. Cards are quicker, easier and less of a commitment than a free download." What this means is that even mobile sites or apps they offer may be outdone by the search engines usage of cards.

Clearly, mobile is really altering how we interact with the Internet, going so far as to change the very face of it. Consumers, according to several studies, will look at their phones around 150 times daily, and with more than two billion phone users, it means that changes brought by mobile are likely to be ongoing.

The Emerging Use of Mobile

A massive Pew study about the use of mobile technology in emerging countries makes this point very clear. Though smart phones are not as common in emerging nations as they are in other locations around the world, owners are using them at a rapidly increasing rate. Texting is the biggest application with social media at a close second (for smartphone owners).

Of interest to marketers however, is this little nugget tucked into the Pew findings, "While the Internet still has a limited reach in the emerging and developing world, once people do gain access to the Internet, they quickly begin to integrate it into their lives. A significant number of people in these nations say they use the Internet on a daily basis, including roughly half of those polled in Lebanon, Russia and Argentina. At least 20% use the Internet daily in 15 of the 24 nations surveyed."

It may be deeply depressing to discover that more people have access to mobile devices than to clean water, but the reality is that mobile devices are a conduit to information and change. After all, the impact of mobile on marketing is profound, but the impact of mobile in terms of information is equally profound.

No matter what message you are seeking to spread via your marketing plans, it is of the utmost importance that mobile, and mobile in terms of its rapid-fire changes, plays a key role. Focus on the visual, the direct, and the fastest downloads possible (after all, 70% of viewers delete messages that don't read well on their device) and you will see that your messages are shared to social media, opened, and responded to through mobile devices more than anything else.

Mobile Websites vs. Mobile Apps: Do You Need Both?

There is a huge difference between an app and a website, and companies of all sizes need to consider whether theirs is a "one or the other" or "both" situation. While it is a given that any organization has to have some accessibility for mobile devices of the Android or Apple varieties, many are unaware of which choice is the best.

To help you make the right call about your company's needs, let's take a moment to compare a mobile website versus mobile apps.

The Differences

A mobile website is one that contains the entire website, and usually means that it has either been entirely redesigned for use on a mobile device or is the end result of responsive design that allows the site to automatically adjust based on the browser. Whether you are using an Apple phone with iOS or Android, responsive design will know what to do to let you see the entire site.

Mobile apps, on the other hand are just that - applications. It must be downloaded like software and then installed before it can be used. It allows a user to access your business and find certain information or solutions, but a website it is not.

The Benefits

If you are wondering if your organization needs both, let's look at the benefits. The mobile website gives a visitor the full deal. It can feature the same content and functions as the website is accessed through a computer. However, the wiser choice is to have it made with responsive design to allow it to appear and function on all devices.

The mobile apps may have a huge array of the same features as the mobile website, but there is one major advantage and that is that the app lives on the user's device. This means it can provide geo-targeted notifications, collect information about the user's behaviors and preferences, and mobile apps can be designed to make it amazingly easy to enjoy things like mobile payment or loyalty programs.

The End Call

So, should you stick with a mobile website or are mobile apps the way of the future? Again, it could be an either-or answer, but in reality there is just one smart course of action for anyone with a business or organization in need of an audience. That answer is to be sure your website is mobile ready with responsive design. But you should also be sure that you have a mobile app in the works or are ready in the near future, if the benefits fit within your desired app user experience.

People are going to look at websites on their mobile devices more than they do on desktop or laptop computers. The shift away from typical computer behavior (even though Google remains king of search engines no matter what you use) shows that most mobile users access almost 51 apps each month and the majority of app usage is limited to the top five apps: Facebook, Instagram, WhatsApp, YouTube and Messenger.

However, it had better be a good one because statistics also reveal that 20% of consumers drop mobile apps that do not function well, and even if they give them a second try, less than 16% go back for a third shot. So troubleshoot any mobile apps long before they are released for loading by your audience or the consumer market.

Mobility is a must, and around 85% of the consumer market has indicated a preference for apps over mobile websites. Still a lot of people like to use browsers and search engines, so accessing a mobile ready website is still a common action too.

It is interesting to consider where these technologies are going, but one certainty is that they are here to stay and your organization must be prepared to respond to whatever direction consumers go. Right now... it looks like there are cases for both.

SMS Marketing

How much texting would you say you do each day? Did that question elicit a whistle or a "phew"? If so, then you already see how and why mobile marketing through SMS/texting is such a vital method for a business to use. Keep in mind, in this section, we will use the terms SMS, texting or both, they all mean the same thing.

According to one study, 2.27 trillion texts are sent each year in the US (that's over 6 billion a day if you were wondering). And how many of those are yours? Around 20 for each person in the US, thus the shift from email marketing to texting/SMS mobile messages. Texts are open 98% of the time and usually within three minutes of receiving. The average teenager/young adult sends over 3300 texts per month.

With the rise of smartphones, it makes more sense than ever for the use of mobile marketing through an SMS. Even more so when you note that a coupon, special offer or other marketing message sent via texting are redeemed around eight times more often than email messages.

Solid Reasons to Keep Mobile and SMS in the Marketing Plan

Mobile marketing, well, that's just a no brainer. After all, most of us are now no farther from our phones than arm's reach. Most people use their phones as their sole source of communication and also in place of a laptop or desktop computer. How many times have you "Googled" something using a phone?

Most of us also use our mobile phones to send texts rather than dialing the actual number. We prefer electronic communications, and that says a great deal about the best choice for marketing messages. Though a lot of us still use all of the standard communication tools that include snail mail, social media, email, and SMS and texting. It is often the text that wins our favor.

The Generation Gaps

And one point of particular interest is that it is the mobile marketing using SMS that seems to generate the most customer loyalty - no matter the generation. For example, accurate targeting is something that all consumers want and need. The teen and the grandfather alike want to get messages that they, well … want. SMS and texting allow recipients to actually subscribe and get the kinds of messages they desire. Unsubscribing is not rocket science either, and is done with one-step.

How often do most consumers wish they could stop receiving mountains of snail mail messages, social media ads and posts, and even emails that have to be tagged to be sent into spam or junk? With the mobile messages sent via texting, though, it is really a matter of getting the news they want to hear. Although, people will block your messages or opt-out if you abuse things and send too many texts.

<u>What Mobile Marketing to Send</u>

To describe mobile via SMS as flexible is putting it lightly. Consider the ways that many organizations and companies are using it globally and locally:

- Mobile coupons
- Texting to win, join, or vote for something
- Sending MMS (which can include audio, video, or images) in addition to text
- Reminding individuals about appointments or groups about events
- Mass messages that all customers can benefit from hearing

Keep in mind that most messages are limited in size to around 160 characters. This is a benefit too, as it forces you to keep mobile messages as concise and pointed as possible. Using text messages as part of your marketing campaign just makes good sense. They have to be brief and that can make it as simple as texting out your call-to-action. There are dozens of ways companies are successfully using this mode of communication, and the statistics continually prove it is the best way to connect.

When Not to Use Texting

While we have talked about numerous ways to use texting as a marketing channel, we have to make sure we address the times that texting should not be used. SMS shouldn't be used for information that needs to be utilized significantly later. Any information sent by text should be readily actionable in a short timeframe. Try to avoid embedding links into SMS for devices in emerging countries where the user might not have a data plan or Wi-Fi to access the link, as this may result in frustrating your customers.

Location Based Experience and Your App

With the rise of the internet of things, Apple iBeacon and Google's geo-features, we will continue to see our mobile devices interact and react to our locations and the things that are around us. From alerts that will pop-up based on our location to ecoupons that arrive when we walk into stores, we will see geolocation play-a-major role in our daily lives. The lines between offline and online will continue to blur and geolocation will play-a-major role in this transition. We will continue to see opportunities where our offline activities impact us online and our online influence will have offline rewards, such as:

- Disney bracelet - Allows Disney to track migration patterns around their Disneyworld park properties, control entrance to the park, payment options and give Disney real-time information on location.

- Walmart - Allows app users to have a different Walmart app experience when inside a physical Walmart versus offsite. Has mapping of each Walmart store and can pinpoint a users location within the store and guide them to their desired product.

Whether we know it or not, many of the world's favorite apps don't bother asking the question and instead use a feature known as geolocation. It is wireless detection of the actual location of a device at any given moment. It lets other people know where we are, but it also allows apps to activate when we enter specific locations.

"The long-anticipated next frontier in mobile technology. They stand to shake-up industries from retail-to-healthcare, by transforming how companies interact with customers…The ability to identify a customer's location at any time opens up seemingly endless sales, marketing and business opportunities." (TechTarget)

Take the example of coffee giant Starbucks. Those who use their app will enjoy automatic use of their loyalty card, find discounts applied, and allow the app to track their preferred drinks. This is essential data that can allow the firm to customize discounts, rewards and perks. Other key retailers who are currently using this feature in their apps are Walmart and Fandango, and consumers generally appreciate the outcomes. Google maps, Uber, Foursquare and a handful of other commonly used apps, including Facebook's check-in features, are due to geolocation as well.

Though some concerns exist where privacy, safety, and security overlap with geolocation (i.e. perhaps you would prefer that someone not know where you are at any given moment) most app users approve. In fact, many are actually coming to depend on it. For example, statistics tell us that 40% of mobile searches have "local intent", and that 70% of mobile searches lead to action within an hour.

Geolocation in the browser or app allows the whole process to be streamlined for targeted results (benefit from a "flash" sale or use an instant discount) to occur.

How Is It Done?

Essentially, geolocation relies on the GPS chip in any smartphone. It uses all available data to locate the exact position. This might be satellite or cell tower triangulation or even Wi-Fi networks to pinpoint the location. Obviously, indoor locations can be more challenging, but the use of Wi-Fi location is how options such as Walmart geolocation occur.

Built in technologies in addition to GPS are ensuring optimal outcomes for developers who opt to use geolocation. Take the Apple iBeacon technology. As one report explained, "If a customer has downloaded an Apple store app and goes into, say, a department store, iBeacon sensors can recognize that the customer has walked in and send special offers to a smartphone or guide the customer to a specific item, among other possibilities." Described as a Bluetooth low-energy (BLE) technology, it relies on actual transmitters in Apple devices to perform the onsite geolocation. Meant to support much better indoor mapping, it is the perfect solution to failures in traditional GPS mapping options.

Those apps that use the Apple iBeacon technology can also be cued by the owner to activate when detected or they can opt-out and simply change permissions. So, the frequent shopper at one location need not feel pestered by ads unless they are eager to hear about all of the deals in the store, and allow their information to be harvested (i.e. what they purchase, and so on).

Of course Apple's iBeacon is not the only way that geolocation is being integrated into apps. There is also the Geolocation API from Google. This is something that allows the browser to know precisely where you are located, and share this information with websites or apps that request it. When using a desktop, you see the pop-up asking for permission to find out your current location. This same tech is what Google geolocation provides, but through the mobile platform. Developers can cue this function in app design and create a much better and far more targeted user experience.

With thc anticipated expansion of mobile audiences by 2020, at which time it is estimated that more than 3 billion devices will be at work, savvy marketers will want to give geolocation serious consideration. Targeted marketing benefits the businesses as well as consumers. After all, truly useful offers or information will be on-hand whenever they enter a building or business in which apps and geolocation are at work.

As a rapidly emerging issue, geolocation is very promising. Due to concerns about privacy, many apps allow opting out. There are also some issues associated with security that need to be addressed, but geolocation is something that all marketers must consider, with almost any app benefitting from its use.

Analytics

When it comes to mobile analytics there are quite a few key things that you should pay attention to. Whether it's your mobile site or your mobile app, the usage patterns and key stats will tell the story of how people interact with your mobile properties. Some of the key areas to pay attention to are:

- Device types - What types of devices are people using most to connect with your mobile property? Is it smartphones, tablets, or another mobile device category that's yet-to-be developed? We are looking at you smart glasses...

- Mobile OS (operating systems) - Whether it's iPhone users or Android users, your organization needs to pay attention to which OS is used most often. Especially if you are deciding to build a mobile app, you can look at the mobile website stats and see which OS is being used and build an app for that OS (iPhone or Android) first, if you have to choose between one or the other.

- Page / App Speed - The speed of mobile site/app is one of the most important aspects of the entire user experience. If a mobile property (site/app) loads slow or has a slow response time to touch, users are more likely to bounce from your site/app and never come back.

- Bounce Rate - One of the key things to track on a mobile site/app is the path that users take while using the property and where they bounce (leave). If you see that users are following a certain path and leaving when they get to a certain page, then you can either guide them to another path or make sure whatever key call-to-action you have is located on the page they get-to when they drop-off.

- Crashes - This is mainly for app users and organizations with an app. Monitoring how often your app crashes and what users are doing to make the app crash is priority when analyzing the user experience for your app. Using tools like Crashlytics, you can see the actions users take on your app and determine what is making it crash and how to fix it.

When it comes to mobile analytics, just like the analytics of all the other digital platforms we have talked about in this book, analyze what you are currently doing, optimize it so that it can be done better and yield better results and then repeat the process.

CHAPTER 8 - INNOVATIVE CONNECTIONS

Innovation - What's Coming Next

As we look at the future of digital platforms, there's a continued shift to making things easier, more integrated and definitely less private. Data has become one of the most valuable resources in the world and every platform we use moving forward will be collecting as much as possible. Unfortunately, as digital platforms move forward and progress, I see many organizations continually playing catch-up. They are already behind the curve when it comes to current technology, and unfortunately are caught off-guard when new technology arrives. This "always behind" approach means organizations are always reacting instead of being proactive. For this reason, I have included this section on innovation. This chapter talks about some emerging technologies that need your attention, as well as ways that you can implement them into your upcoming digital strategies.

Mobile - More than phones

There's another point I want to focus on within this chapter as well. When organizations think of mobile, they think of mobile phones, and that's not necessarily wrong. Unfortunately, it's short-sighted because mobile consists of so much more. I genuinely believe that the future of mobile will evolve with wearables and devices we talk to. This will come about with the mass rollout of 5G internet speeds which are looking at 10GB upload and 20GB download over the air. As we get more mobile devices (wearables, audible and IOT) that are connected to this upgraded hyper speed wireless internet, we will start to see more digital platforms emerge that take advantage of this technology. Let's look at a few examples.

Alexa Is Growing and Becoming a Go-To Marketing Platform

People tend to love technology and it is advancing at an unprecedented rate. It was only a couple of decades ago that "beepers" were one of the most advanced pieces of tech that people had. Then along came cellphones and smartphones that changed the way communication and marketing worked. Now, with the advent of basic artificial intelligence that can be brought into the home for a small sum, marketing is going to be changing and adapting once again.

<u>Why Is Alexa Likely to Be the AI of Choice?</u>

While Siri might have been around for longer, most people are finding that Alexa is the go-to choice when it comes to AI that they will have in their home, even if they have an iPhone or iPad with Siri. There are plenty of reasons that this is the case.

Alexa is from Amazon, and the AI has open APIs (application programming interfaces), which means that it is easy for Alexa to be integrated into other devices and not just those made by Amazon. For example, Lenovo came out with a device that can run Alexa. Many devices today are being built to work well with Alexa from companies like Samsung, LG, and even Ford. This has helped to increase the adoption rate of the system.

Of course, Amazon is a massive online retailer, and they have plenty of their own devices that run Alexa, such as the Echo and their Kindle Fire devices. Because Amazon is a household name at this point, Alexa already had brand recognition the moment it was revealed to the world. Adoption has been steady.

Another reason that people have adapted and started to use Alexa more and more is that they like the ability to use their voice as a means to quickly and easily get information and control the system. It is even possible to place orders to Amazon through Alexa.

The system continues to learn and improve, as well, which means better voice recognition, fewer mistakes, and more potential for the future. However, this also means that companies will need to learn how to market for the future and how to make the most out of Alexa.

What Does This Mean for Your Marketing Efforts?

If you are going to be marketing and advertising through Alexa, you need to realize that it is an audio-only medium, which is likely quite different from your other marketing efforts. You have to think very carefully about the language you use to create the right mental images since you will not be able to rely on actual images of products. Your branding must grow to include taglines, branded sound effects and music, and quality voice talent.

Even though this is a new medium, the type of advertising we are talking about has been around for quite some time. Think about the radio advertisements that you have heard. Which ones were effective and which ones did not work? You will want to consider similar types of audio ads if you hope to be effective with this type of marketing.

How Smartwatches Are Used in Marketing

While smartwatches might not be as prevalent as smartphones, they are still quite popular, and more and more people are starting to use them as the years go by. This means that companies should be spending efforts trying to market their brand to smartwatch users just like they do with other mobile users. Of course, the screens on these devices are quite small, and many may not understand just how marketing would even work on these screens. Let's look at a couple of the ways that you could start to use smartwatches in marketing.

Make Sure You Have Content for a Smaller Screen

Because of the size of the screens, you will need to find ways that you can present information in a small, compact format. Typically, this can be done with a single small picture or a short phrase. In some cases, the two can be combined, but you will need to make sure that the phrase is legible whether it is used with or without a picture. You will need to have a different kind of content for people to see on watches when compared with phones.

Less is More

One of the other marketing tips that you will want to consider when working with smartwatches is that people do not want to see an advertisement every single time they look down at their watch or try to do something. They do not want to be sent constant notifications either. The "less is more" approach can work well with this type of marketing, or any type of marketing for that matter. You do not want your ads to be seen as invasive because that will give you a bad name amongst people who see those ads.

It Won't Result in Instant Sales

People who are on their phones and who see advertisements that interest them are more likely to make a purchase than someone who sees an ad on a smartwatch. This is because they can easily use their phone to go to your website and then learn more and decide to buy or not. With a watch, it's different. They are not going to be able to get to your full-site through the watch, so you will need to make sure you have a memorable and easy-to-understand ad that will make them want to return to your site later.

However, if you have an app that is available on the phone, and the ad leads to the app, it could be possible to make fast sales. You need to have an app developed for the watch first, of course, and that might be out of the reach of some marketers.

There is always a learning curve when it comes to marketing. When brick and mortar companies went from using traditional marketing methods to advertising online for desktops and laptops, there were growing pains. The same is true when companies started to advertise on smartphones and tablets, which have smaller screens. It will take time to perfect marketing with smart watches, but it is certainly possible and something that should be pursued.

VR / AR (Virtual Reality / Augmented Reality)

What Is Virtual Reality?

The most basic answer is that it is a three dimensional computer generated setting or environment that can be explored by someone using the appropriate equipment. That equipment, thus far, includes a special-head mounted display or HMD that can display the "world" they are interacting with it. There must also be some sort of input or sensory gear that may include hand mounted controls. Is it the same as augmented reality? Yes and no.

What Is Augmented Reality?

According to most definitions, augmented reality is an integration of the real environment along with digital information or live video. In essence, augmented reality blends an existing picture and adds new information. This requires software and does not feature the same goggles and sensory tech as virtual reality. Most of us are already using this technology with things like online maps, GPS displays, and "virtual" shopping that allows us to upload a photo and "try on" clothes or hairstyles.

The Realities of These Realities

So, we already have some forms of augmented reality available to consumers. Also, virtual reality exists in many spaces, but it is the consumer market that are most eager to see the equipment and technologies for virtual reality expand. Right now, we already use our mobile phones for some forms of augmented reality. The success of games like

Pokémon Go have shown that augmented reality can have mass appeal. Additionally, in scientific, corporate, training and other settings, augmented reality has many proven cases where it is beneficial. Likewise, in 2019, Facebook released Oculus Quest, which follows the previous releases of Oculus Go and Oculus Rift. Each of these devices is another step in the creation of mass appeal VR devices.

Mainstream Ready?

Does all of this mean that virtual reality is ready for the mainstream? If you take the word of industry experts and enthusiasts, few would agree that it is refined enough to satisfy the consumer market. Describing it as still in its infancy or under development, most also agree that it is a technology whose time has come.

Today, these technologies are mostly of specific interest to gamers who have already experienced some form of it at conventions and in specialty settings. Marketers should also take note and consider the ways it may be integrated into any sort of campaigns in the coming years.

We are getting quite close to the next phase of mobile, where smart glasses that can add a digital layer to everything we see, will be the norm. These glasses will use high speed internet (5G), audio voice controls (like Alexa, Google Assistant, Siri) and augmented reality to create immersive environments everywhere we go. We all understand that augmented reality and virtual reality are on the horizon. Advances have already occurred, but the day when you can strap on goggles and enter your favorite fantasy world are still a bit in the future, but just a bit.

Second Screen Experience

Studies have now shown that around 85% of mobile device owners will use their devices while watching TV. Not exactly multi-tasking, it is, as described by the website Mashable: "The use of an additional monitor (e.g. tablet, smartphone) while watching television. It allows the audience to interact with what they're consuming whether it's a TV show, video game or movie."

And just as interesting is what Google has discovered about this trend, namely that, "More than one-fifth (22%) of these consumers are using the TV and their second device in ways that complement each other, even if it is only a simple search related to the live TV programming."

So, you like that actor who played a minor role, you grab the tablet, head to IMdB.com and look at what other films he or she has done. Then you use that information to stream content at a later time or search your cable menu for their name and any shows upcoming in the schedule.

However, as anyone might automatically assume, the most popular way that devices are used is to comment about what it is they are watching. Whether it is the latest episode of "The Walking Dead", a Presidential speech or debate, or the final game of The World Series, people are on Twitter and Facebook making comments, showing screen grabs, and keeping those in their social media networks up to date about everything.

Thus, you see "what's trending" as an almost mirror image on whatever hot programs are running in that time slot, and you see them remain as that same program airs in all time zones across the country. However, the ongoing streams of Facebook and Twitter comments are what make many actually avoid social media in the days after some shows air because they don't want to stumble across "spoilers" if they haven't seen the latest episode.

Is It a Real Thing?

Does this mean that the second screen experience is something that developers are looking closely at? Yes indeed it does. Since the emergence of apps, developers have considered what the trend in "multi-screen" might mean. Google has even done a very formal study, giving the ways we multi-screen official names. They are "sequential" where we move from one device to another in order to complete a goal. For example, you see a car ad on your phone and head to the desktop to do further research. Then there is the simultaneous multi-screener who uses two devices at once. The report said this about it, "we found that TV no longer commands our undivided attention, with 77% of viewers watching TV with another device in hand. In many cases people search on their devices, inspired by what they see on TV." (Google)

Developments in Second Screen Apps

Though it is in the very early days where second screen apps for TV are concerned, the related industries are already exploring the market. After all, there are many direct mentions of cross-platform activities such as online contests that require live TV viewing in order to participate. And one blogger itemized things already done in response to the trends, saying: "Syncing technologies like Auto Content Recognition (ACR) were created, allowing the mobile device to listen to and then sync to the TV experience, while Social TV offerings have continued to mature in functionality and popularity the last couple of years." (PossibleMobile)

On the heels of the earliest innovations, there are communication tools such as the yap.TV app that provides mobile device users with the means of engaging with Facebook and Twitter in order to get specific TV feeds. There are also TV network and TV program specific apps that enable direct interaction and bonus features available strictly through social media.

Understanding Second Screen Right Now

However, it is relevant for any marketers or industry experts to understand that the second screen experience is still a bit blunted. The reasons are many, and among the most important is that the apps being designed to enhance the whole second screen experience seem to be coming from a foundation of revenue generation and advertising rather than engagement. As one expert wrote, "Second screen was born out of boredom and defined by consumers … many apps are coming from advertisers who are side-tracked by pushing their show/product." (PossibleMobile) This falls directly in-line with the other challenge, which is that those responsible for second screen are striving to make it a first screen experience instead. The apps cannot demand constant focus, but only limited interaction or engagement. This is why bonus content, contests, and post-program content seem to be the most successful.

The statistics about app use in general seem to be overlooked by second screen app developers too. With mobile device owners preferring to use only a few of the apps they download, it would be more sensible for networks to create single apps, as opposed to individual apps for each program. There are efforts underway for such solutions, but a true second screen experience must be as brief and least distracting if it is to boost TV popularity. Choosing the show's direction, participating in a quiz, guessing the next play the team is going to run, that's what the players in the TV space need to be focusing on to push this movement to the masses. And developers are doing all they can to accomplish just that, and the masses are showing signs of approval.

SOURCES

- http://venturebeat.com/2013/05/08/five-reasons-you-should-be-using-sms-based-marketing/
- http://eventualmillionaire.com/how-to-get-your-podcast-into-new-and-noteworthy-in-itunes/
- http://cashflowpodcasting.com/how-to-submit-a-podcast-to-google-play-music/
- http://www.apple.com/itunes/podcasts/specs.html
- http://contentmarketinginstitute.com/2012/01/podcasts-content-marketing-strategy/
- http://www.copyblogger.com/why-start-podcast/
- http://www.entrepreneurs-journey.com/230/what-is-a-podcast/
- http://mashable.com/category/second-screen/
- http://www.visionmobile.com/blog/2012/09/from-mobile-to-tv-the-companion-screens-opportunity-and-the-role-of-apps/
- http://googlemobileads.blogspot.com/2012/08/navigating-new-multi-screen-world.html
- http://mashable.com/2014/02/03/second-screen-tv-apps/#zgtYESY8gqqp
- https://possiblemobile.com/2013/04/5-reasons-why-second-screen-has-yet-to-go-mainstream/
- http://www.entrepreneur.com/article/250092
- http://www.forbes.com/sites/jacobmorgan/2014/05/13/simple-explanation-internet-things-that-anyone-can-understand/2/
- http://www.forbes.com/sites/markfidelman/2015/03/26/three-things-you-probably-didnt-know-about-the-future-of-iot/
- http://recode.net/2016/00/21/no-more-waiting-its-time-for-consumer-virtual-reality/
- http://www.wsj.com/articles/virtual-reality-is-taking-its-time-becoming-a-consumer-reality-1420561894
- http://www.digitaltrends.com/mobile/16-percent-of-mobile-userstry-out-a-buggy-app-more-than-twice/
- http://marketingland.com/the-real-impact-of-mobile-on-marketing-more-visual-content-49463
- http://www.pewglobal.org/2014/02/13/emerging-nations-embrace-internet-mobile-technology/
- http://www.dailymail.co.uk/sciencetech/article-2449632/How-check-phone-The-average-person-does-110-times-DAY-6-seconds-evening.html
- http://www.digitaltrends.com/mobile/16-percent-of-mobile-userstry-out-a-buggy-app-more-than-twice/
- https://biteable.com/blog/tips/video-marketing-statistics/
- https://www.wordstream.com/blog/ws/2019/04/04/ecommerce-statistics
- https://www.nptechforgood.com/2018/03/20/10-must-know-stats-about-online-fundraising/
- https://www.oberlo.com/blog/ecommerce-statistics-guide-your-strategy
- https://www.socialmediatoday.com/news/10-social-media-statistics-you-need-to-know-in-2019-infographic/559181/
- https://www.leveragestl.com/social-media-infographic/
- https://chambermaster.com/articles/social-media-stories-for-chambers/
- https://www.clickz.com/the-rise-of-stories-and-the-changing-face-of-social-marketing/214311/
- https://smartwatches.org/learn/strategies-market-your-brand-on-a-smartwatch/
- https://enveritasgroup.com/campfire/challenges-smart-watch-marketing/
- https://www.fastcompany.com/3068721/the-real-reasons-that-amazons-alexa-may-become-the-go-to-ai-for-the-home
- https://www.forbes.com/sites/peterhorst/2017/06/19/6-ways-to-master-marketing-in-a-world-of-siri-alexa/#88312676053e
- https://www.wareable.com/features/alexa-winning-smart-home-war-7778
- https://newmediaservices.com.au/benefits-of-social-media-engagement/
- https://buffer.com/library/social-media-engagement
- https://www.internetconsultancy.pro/blog/the-power-of-paid-advertising-on-social-media/
- http://www.customerexperienceinsight.com/why-amazons-service-is-so-good-and-how-yours-can-be-too/
- https://quoracreative.com/article/mobile-marketing-statistics
- http://searchcrm.techtarget.com/feature/Location-based-apps-present-opportunities-and-data-challenges
- http://mobilemarketingengine.com/23-mobile-marketing-stats/
- http://www.techhive.com/article/192803/geolo.html
- http://www.zdnet.com/article/what-is-apple-ibeacon-heres-what-you-need-to-know/
- https://blog.hubspot.com/marketing/what-is-digital-marketing

ABOUT THE AUTHOR

Jason Caston is an international speaker, author, professor and digital/social platform specialist for faith-based organizations. Having helped train more than 5000 leaders and built websites, apps and social media properties that reach over 8 million people daily, Caston has proven that his cutting-edge technological savvy and business acumen have made him a sought after Digital Platforms, Internet Church, Mobile and Social Media Specialist. Caston has developed an innovative approach to helping organizations advance their online presence using a five-part approach of Websites, multimedia, eCommerce, Social Media and Mobile. Caston has authored more than 10 books, including The iChurch Method series on establishing a digital presence and Social Connections book on Social Media for Organizations. Additionally, Caston is the Director of Digital Media at Daystar TV and the spokesperson for AT&T national #InspiredMobility campaign that highlights how we use mobile technology to enhance our spiritual and personal lives. Connect with him on Twitter and Instagram @jasoncaston.

Made in United States
North Haven, CT
14 May 2024

52509361R00063